Mansfield

IN OLD PHOTOGRAPHS

Church Street at the turn of the century.

Mansfield

IN OLD PHOTOGRAPHS

Compiled by DAVID CRUTE,
BARBARA GALLON,
MICHAEL J. JACKSON AND
ALBERT WOOLLEY
OLD MANSFIELD SOCIETY

Budding
BOOKS

A Budding Book

First published in 1993 by Alan Sutton
Publishing Limited

This edition published in 1998 by Budding Books,
an imprint of Sutton Publishing Limited
Phoenix Mill · Thrupp · Stroud · Gloucestershire
GL5 2BU

Dedicated to the memory of Albert Sorby Buxton,
John Harrop White, Daniel H. Maltby and the
other founder members of the Old Mansfield
Society.

A catalogue record for this book is available from
the British Library

ISBN 1-84015-048-3

Typesetting and origination by
Sutton Publishing Limited.
Printed in Great Britain by
WBC Limited, Bridgend, Mid-Glamorgan.

Contents

Introduction

When Miss Susannah Parsons, the proprietress of one of Mansfield's private schools, posed for her photograph in 1862 (p. 78), it is unlikely that there were many cameras in the town. Most, if not all of them were used for portraiture; rarely were they taken from the studio into the streets. Any impressions of the appearance of the town of that time, of its buildings, of the activities of its people, come from the pencil and brush of the artist. Most renowned of these was Mr J. Seddon Tyrer, headmaster of the School of Art from its beginnings in 1871, and there were others. By the close of the century, however, the number of cameras in Mansfield had increased. Several professional photographers, of whom Mr George Ellis of the Britannia Studio was the best known, had set up in business. Formally posed, starched and stiff in their Sunday best, local society from the highest to the humblest was pictured for posterity by their lenses. Out of doors they were no less busy, recording special events, notable visits, spectacular happenings; in fact, anything that would draw a crowd. Some of these pictures illustrated the local papers, others were produced as postcards which reached their height of popularity in the years preceding the First World War.

At the same time improvements in camera design were being made. Smaller models that were simpler to operate were becoming increasingly available, a major development occurring in 1900 when the first Kodak Brownie appeared in the shops. No longer was photography an expensive, complicated procedure, practised only by the professional and an occasional amateur. The Brownie brought in the age of the snapshot and the family album, recording the birthday and anniversary, the outing and holiday.

This collection of photographs has been selected from both these sources, the carefully composed study of the professional and the casual, spur of the moment snap. They span more than 120 years and form the largest number of pictures of the town ever to appear in one book. When the first one was taken just over 10,000 people lived in Mansfield, most of them along streets clustered within a few minutes' walk of the Market Place. Although the town was essentially industrial, with its textile mills, foundries, maltings and various smaller workshops, it still retained much of the atmosphere of a market town. The countryside was close by, livestock was driven to and from the cattle market, farmers' wives spread out their dairy produce for sale, and carriers' carts brought in visitors from the surrounding villages. Although smoke from an increasing number of chimneys may have begun to darken the sky, the whiff of the farm yard still pervaded many of its streets.

Change dominated the succeeding years. The population increased sixfold and new houses spread outwards, covering much of the open countryside that had previously separated the town from its nearest neighbours of Pleasley, Mansfield Woodhouse and Sutton-in-Ashfield. Most of this new building was of brick, contrasting with that of traditional local stone and the few surviving examples of earlier timber frame construction. Although some of these older houses still stand they are comparatively few. Neglect and redevelopment, some of it insensitive, have taken their toll, the latter often to the visual detriment of the townscape, though in the 1990s a more sympathetic attitude is apparent.

While some of the industries that were working in the early years covered by this book still exist, others have disappeared to be replaced by different means of manufacture and new sources of employment. Brewing still flourishes though the last working malt kiln now houses a night-club. Textile and hosiery production have almost ceased; mills that once reverberated to the throb of the loom and the rattle of the knitting machine are now silent. Some, indeed, have been demolished, others converted to different uses, while the remainder stand gaunt and derelict, an invitation to trespass and vandalism. By the turn of the century Mansfield was assuming the appearance and atmosphere of a mining town. Although no collieries were actually sunk within the borough boundaries, the town was surrounded by mines, two so close that their galleries have burrowed beneath its streets and houses to the extent that subsidence has been, and still is, a serious concern for many people. Miners formed a substantial part of the local work force; they and their families made major contributions to the town's economy, its civic, social and sporting life. Already pit closures have threatened this involvement and it remains to be seen how the future re-organization of the industry will affect the district.

For many visitors the most vivid visual memory of the town is of the railway viaduct that bestrides its centre. Today only an occasional coal train rumbles across its solid arches, though when it was built in the early 1870s traffic was much heavier. Passenger trains ran to and from Worksop while goods trains carrying a variety of freight were a regular sight. The Midland station was the hub of a web of branch lines that radiated in all directions to link with the main line system and carry Mansfield people to the four corners of the land. By the 1890s, on each weekday close on one hundred passenger trains called at the station. Now there is none although hopes of restoring some services in the near future are reasonably optimistic.

On the roads the horse has given way to the internal combustion engine though there have been two interesting variations on the way. The first was experimental, lasted but a short time and was soon regarded as a failure. It was a steam bus, appropriately called 'The Pioneer', which after a few months of fitful service and frequent breakdowns was abandoned. The second was longer lasting and though far from comfortable and somewhat accident prone was affectionately regarded by many and now enjoys an almost mythological status. This was the town's tramway system, which was inaugurated in 1905 and ran until 1932. Thereafter the car, the lorry and the motor bus gained an ever increasing ascendancy until their numbers have proved too much for a road layout that evolved for far lighter and much slower traffic. Whether the eventual completion of the inner ring road will bring appreciable relief, only time will tell.

Few, if any, of Miss Susannah Parson's contemporaries had a bathroom in their homes; all had to make use of a privy in their yard or garden and every drop of water they used was raised by a pump or drawn from a well. Just as the appearance of the town has changed so radically over the years, so has the way of life of its inhabitants. Poorly built, insanitary and cramped housing has been swept away to be replaced by large housing estates of the inter- and post-war years. Nowadays every child goes to school though far fewer people attend church or chapel. As the average working day has shortened the ways of occupying leisure time have increased. Those available a hundred years ago can soon be listed: a little sport, an occasional concert, a country walk, an hour in the garden or at the public house just about summarizes the choice. Today the scope is much wider though still insufficient to satisfy the inclinations and demands of some people.

Whatever the pattern of everyday life might have been, external events have frequently influenced it. Warfare has taken local menfolk to the South African veldt, the mud and squalor of the Western Front, the North African desert, the jungles of Burma and the D-Day beaches. Meanwhile, those at home have had to adjust to the stringencies of food rationing, the wailing of the air raid siren and the constant worry about the fate of loved ones in the forces. Happier memories, however, tend to prevail and, from time to time, occasions of great rejoicing have packed the Market Place. Perhaps the most notable of these was on 14 July 1891 when the town celebrated its grant of borough status. On that day, so it was reported, about 8,000 people managed to squeeze into the square to give vocal support to what many of them could neither see nor hear. Royal visits have brought out the crowds too. The town was similarly thronged to greet King George V and Queen Mary in 1914 and the present Queen in 1977.

The changing town, its people, their homes and way of life, their work and means of transport, their high days, holidays and moments of leisure have all been captured by the camera. The pictures that follow are but a selection chosen from thousands that were made available to the compilers of the book. Most of these came from local archive collections while the rest were taken from family albums. Some of the latter have been hidden away in drawers and cupboards for many years and there is no doubt that many more still remain in such concealment. While they are there they are at least safe, though in days to come they may be at risk of the bonfire or the bin. This would be a shame for much of interest would then be lost. A glance through these pages shows the value and fascination of such pictures and should any be in danger of destruction it would be beneficial if they were offered to such organizations as the Old Mansfield Society, the Mansfield Museum or the Local Studies Department of the library. There they will be preserved and available for future reference and use.

SECTION ONE
Topography

Stockwell Gate, 1956. On the left is the Empire cinema, which closed in January 1961, and opposite is the Belle Vue Inn. In the background can be seen the old clock tower of the Co-operative stores.

The Rushley Inn was unthought of when this photograph of the Nottingham Road and Old Derby Road junction was taken around 1920. A horse-drawn cart could travel at a leisurely pace on an empty highway still edged with lime trees planted in the previous century. In the left distance is Robin Down Hill, with very few houses to be seen. In October 1929 the Old Derby Road was closed at the top and renamed Forest Hill.

With a single tram, a solitary cyclist and one or two pedestrians, no one seems in a particular hurry on this Edwardian summer's day on Nottingham Road. The turreted Cattle Market house was designed by the Mansfield-born though Nottingham-based architect Watson Fothergill. The only other example of his work in the town was the Congregational chapel on Westgate that closed in 1981 and was subsequently demolished. There is no sign in this picture of the United Methodist chapel. This was not built until 1913.

Woodhouse Road was a prestigious area in which to build in the late nineteenth and early twentieth centuries. Many of Mansfield's prosperous businessmen owned large houses set in pleasant gardens here, while smaller stone or brick terrace or semi-detached dwellings catered for more modest incomes. In the top photograph the gates of Queen Elizabeth's Girls' School are on the left. Below is a 1926 photograph showing clearly how road widening had removed many fine trees.

This view of the end of Westgate shows two eye-catching edifices of bygone Mansfield. One is the cast iron, dome-capped gentlemen's urinal in the centre of the picture. Though demolished with little thought years ago, such objects are now preserved in folk museums. The second building of special note is the Congregational chapel, built in 1878 to plans by Watson Fothergill. Its opening ceremony was unusual. The windows were still unglazed and as the day was showery the service was occasionally interrupted as the ladies raised their umbrellas.

Westgate House was a private residence retaining a front garden, gates and railings when this photograph was taken in 1926. The tall staircase window was a feature seen in many late Georgian houses in the town. This type of smooth ashlar construction has weathered well and, in spite of its commercial use as a restaurant today, the house has retained much of its façade unchanged. Miss Susannah Parsons would have no difficulty in recognizing her school building.

Westgate was unusually tranquil when this photograph was taken in the 1880s. On the left was Dr Godfrey's house, the upper windows of which remain unchanged today. On the right, the recently rebuilt Nag's Head public house stood next to the home of Mr W.E. Baily of Mansfield Brewery Co. When the Nag's Head was demolished in the 1970s, seventeenth-century windows in adjacent premises were exposed.

Westgate, 1913. The erection of the new premises for the opticians, Gray & Selby, at No. 27, next door to the butchers shop of Richard Blythe at No. 29. Gray & Selby (later Gray & Bull) remained in occupation till the 1960s, while the last occupants – from the late 1960s to the demolition in the early 1970s which resulted in the Four Seasons Shopping Centre – were Wigfalls.

Carter Lane was one of many streets built up in the late nineteenth and early twentieth centuries with red-brick, mainly terrace housing, some of which covered the sites of the Rock Hill Windmills. On the right of this photograph, dated 1920, is Mr A.H. Smith's billiard saloon, established in 1914. Pedestrians walking in the road at this point today would be risking life and limb as this is a busy junction.

Market Street in 1913. On the left was Jolly's, the tobacconist, with Jolly's, the jeweller, immediately below. On the opposite side was Richardson's Remnant Store and Bosworth's butchers, now the Vanity Box.

Park Avenue in 1905. Park Avenue was developed in the late nineteenth and early twentieth centuries, on land which was copyhold of the Manor of Mansfield. Known as The Park at that time, these solid stone houses were inhabited by professional and business men and their families. Along with Crow Hill and Woodhouse Road, this was a very select part of the town in which to own a house.

Albert House, Bridge Street, *c.* 1900. The 'doorway' on the right is in fact the entrance to an alley leading to a yard at the rear of Albert House and the adjacent Elm Tree Inn. The Elm Tree Inn was demolished around 1903, whereupon Albert House, which had been a lodging house, became the new Elm Tree Inn until it too was demolished in 1966.

The Forest Stone stands in a field off the old Newark Road, marking the site of the ancient Swainmote Court held here when Mansfield was within the Royal Forest of Sherwood. Thrice each year the Steward of the Swainmote, the Officers of the Forest and the Lord Chief Justice in Eyre met here to adjudicate upon offences such as the poaching of the King's deer and encroachment upon the Forest. After the Moot held on Holyrood day the company rode into Mansfield, where the verderers held a feast at either the Swan Inn or the Old Eclipse.

Mansfield Cemetery was opened in December 1857 on a twenty-acre site laid out by local architect Mr Charles Neale, who planted fine specimen trees and provided there the first asphalt paths in the town. The lodges, chapels and gates were designed by J.P. Pritchett and Sons of York, who specialized in cemetery buildings. Before the town had a public park the cemetery was a popular place for courting couples on summer evenings.

Colonel Thomas Wildman's tomb was designed by T.C. Hine of Nottingham. The Colonel, who was a Waterloo hero, died in 1859. He was one of the wealthiest men to be buried in the cemetery.

The junction of Littleworth, Church Lane and Brunts Street, photographed around 1905 from a point on Weighbridge Road leading to the Gas and Electricity works. The buildings behind the central pole mark the site of the present day Dove and Redferns' garage and were then part of the stables and coach house of Grove House.

The redevelopment of the town centre. The draft for the development was first published in May 1963, and here, in 1973, we see the extensive clearance work, which preceded the building of the Four Seasons Shopping Centre, in progress. In the centre background is St John's church, while on the extreme left is the rear end of the Rosemary Centre. The Four Seasons Shopping Centre was opened on 9 March 1976.

Berry Hill Hall, seen here in 1900, was originally built in the 1750s, and was enlarged and improved by successive owners. The façade was remodelled in 1889 when the hall passed to the Hollins of Pleasley Vale. Sir Edward Walker, owner from 1850 until 1872, was knighted by Queen Victoria when he was mayor of Chester at the time of the birth of the Prince of Wales in 1841. Mrs Laetitia Hollins sold the hall in 1920 and it became a rehabilitation hospital for injured mine workers. In 1993 the building is empty and vandalized, awaiting redevelopment.

This fine wrought-iron gate separated the flower garden of Grove House, Brunts Street, from the adjacent paddock. Built as a manor house in the early eighteenth century and enlarged during the nineteenth, Grove House was an Academy for Boys, and then the town house of W.J. Chadburn of Mansfield Brewery Co., who no doubt found the proximity of the house to his business premises very convenient. In 1919 the Duke of Portland gave it to St Peter's church for use as a parish centre. The house was demolished in 1977.

The Hermitage around 1920. In the thirteenth century Thomas Bek, Bishop of St David's and a tenant of the King in the Manor of Mansfield, established a summer dwelling and sanatorium for monks on Mansfield moor known as 'Esthwaite Ermitage'. The name is remembered in Hermitage Mill and the house known as the Hermitage which still stands although the cottages shown here have gone.

SECTION TWO
Personalities

'Chad' Allen, seen here in 1926, was a prominent local swimmer who was later manager of Mansfield Baths.

Mr John Maltby, born in 1806, followed for more than fifty years the vocation of schoolmaster in the academy he established in Rock Court in 1836. He married in 1830 and had fifteen children, of whom the youngest was Daniel H. Maltby. Mr Maltby was said to be a splendid disciplinarian and few boys left his school without great proficiency in arithmetic and penmanship. He was an ardent Wesleyan and his activities in the Reform movement led to his expulsion in 1849. In the Reformed church, he was Sunday School Superintendent until his death in 1886.

Alderman Daniel H. Maltby assisted his father at the Rock Court Academy until he succeeded as headmaster in 1886. Three years later the school moved to Clerkson Street where it continued until July 1928 after ninety-two years. From 1897 until his death in February 1938 Mr Maltby was connected with civic life. Twice mayor of Mansfield, he was made an Honorary Freeman of the Borough in 1932. He was a founder member of the Old Mansfield Society, a member of the County Cricket Club and a trustee of several charities. Like his father he was a Methodist who played the organ and was a local preacher.

The Sixth Duke of Portland and his bride, the former Miss Winifred Dallas-Yorke, shortly after their marriage in June 1889. The Duke was Lord of the Manor of Mansfield and this traditional role was exercised in many ways in the wider industrial sphere which increasingly surrounded him. He was particularly generous to the town of Mansfield and his wife, who died in 1954, worked energetically for Harlow Wood Hospital and for animal welfare.

John Harrop White was born in the Swan Hotel in 1856 and he was to feature prominently in the affairs of Mansfield until his death in 1951. Receiving his education at Grove House School and Old Trafford, he began his professional career as a solicitor in 1878. At the early age of 26 he was elected a town's commissioner and in 1891 a member of Mansfield's first Town Council. Town clerk and mayor in 1924, Harrop White devoted his life to his native town, which acknowledged this by awarding him the Freedom of the Borough.

Mr Frank H. Jessop was a solicitor by profession though a musician by inclination. For a time he was director of the Mansfield Amateur Operatic Society and also chairman of the Mansfield and District Music Club but he was best known as organist and choirmaster of Bridge Street Methodist chapel. He held this position from 1920 until 1959. A young man whose work brought him to Mansfield asked a colleague where he could hear the best church music. 'Go to Bridge Street' was the immediate reply.

Although Harry Penson earned his living at the Mansfield Shoe Co., his real life began when his daily work was over. He was a man of the theatre and was never happier than when acting, directing and writing plays. In the 1920s he joined the Robin Hood Players who performed at the Westfield Folk House and also took part in the productions of the Mansfield Operatic Society. Here he is seen as Squire Weston in *Tom Jones*, their show of 1927. Today, he is best remembered as the founder of the Penson Players who, from their beginnings in 1948, have brought great pleasure to local playgoers.

John Ogdon was born on 27 January 1937 at Mansfield Woodhouse but it was in Mansfield that he took his first lesson in playing the piano. His teacher was Miss Nellie Houseley and it was she who first recognized his outstanding talent and laid the foundation of discipline and technique so necessary for its full development. After studying at the Royal Manchester College of Music his career began dramatically when, taking the place of an indisposed artist, the sheer brilliance of his playing astounded the audience. The climax of his skill and virtuosity came in 1962 when he was declared a joint winner of the prestigious Tchaikovsky competition in Moscow. Thereafter, illness tended to limit his career though it did nothing to diminish his genius. Sadly, he died on 1 August 1989. John Ogdon always retained a warm affection for Mansfield, visiting the town quite regularly and delighting local audiences with his playing. Perhaps the most memorable of these occasions was in 1983 when he accompanied the Mansfield Choral Society in a performance of Franz Liszt's oratorio *Christus*. This photograph was taken shortly afterwards and shows John Ogdon sitting beside Pamela Cook, founder and conductor of the widely acclaimed Cantamus Choir and, behind him, David Chamberlain, conductor of the Choral Society, and the four soloists.

SECTION THREE

Industry

The Mansfield Brewery, seen from the end of Brunts Street in 1929. It was established in 1855 and the premises, seen here, were opened in May 1908.

Field Mill was built in the late eighteenth century by the Duke of Portland as one of several water-powered mills along the Maun to stimulate the local textile trade and offer alternative employment at a time of economic depression in the frame-work knitting industry – the main cottage industry of the town at that time. Occupied by Messrs Greenhalgh for most of the last century, it was badly damaged by fire in 1901 and remained disused until its demolition in 1925.

M.G. & A. Bradley occupied the old and new Town Mills on Bridge Street. They became a subsidiary of the Fine Cotton Spinning and Doubling Association Ltd and remained in business until 1956. Both mills were derelict for many years until the new Town Mill was demolished in 1987 while the old Town Mill was converted into a public house in 1988.

'Buster' Linney in the cotton doubling firm of Harwood Cash & Co. Ltd, Lawn Mills, Rosemary Street, around 1950. He was a son-in-law of the founder, John Harwood Cash, who started the firm in 1906. The firm was very successful and by the time it was taken over by Courtaulds in 1973 the annual turnover was around £15 million and the total number of employees was about 1,000. The takeover was not a success, however, and Lawn Mills was closed within a few years, to re-open in 1984 as the Rosemary Centre.

Stanton Mill was built on Bath Lane at the beginning of the nineteenth century by Charles Stanton as a water-powered textile mill. Charles Stanton also had Carr Bank House built at about the same time. He later sold both to the Duke of Portland, who in turn leased them to Herbert Greenhalgh who went on to expand his textile business to include Field Mill and Little Matlock Mill by the mid-nineteenth century.

Jackson's Mill. In the late eighteenth century, there were no fewer than eight windmills standing on the high ground on the eastern side of the town. Jackson's Mill, erected in 1779, was a 'smock' mill, built in brick, conical in shape, with a wooden revolving cap and a fantail which turned the cap to take advantage of wind changes. At one time it was owned by a Friendly Society and members were able to grind their own corn. It fell into dereliction in the early 1920s.

Frame-work knitter. The frame-work knitting machine was invented in 1589 by William Lee of Calverton and developed to form one of the county's staple industries up to the mid-nineteenth century. The frame-work knitters or 'stockingers' as they were called, after the product made by the frames, were required to work long hours for little reward in rooms with large, high windows to let in as much daylight as possible. Towards the top left of the picture above can be seen a glass bowl suspended from the ceiling. This would be filled with water to focus the last rays of daylight on to the frame, and so extend the working day as far as possible without recourse to the expense of candles. In the early nineteenth century technical developments of the frame, combined with low wages, gave rise to the term, 'Luddite', after desperate stockingers fought to maintain their livelihoods. In Mansfield the waters of Cauldwell Dam became notorious as their last despairing refuge, while the road up Peck's Hill was built by unemployed stockingers in an early example of 'work fair'.

The brewery, seen from the end of Meadow Walk in 1908. The prominent feature is the tall structure of the brewhouse. In the foreground is a rare shot of the brewery wine and spirit shop, long since demolished. In the 1920s, in the days of home baking, it was a common sight to see the local children carrying jugs, heading for the brewery, for threepennyworth of yeast.

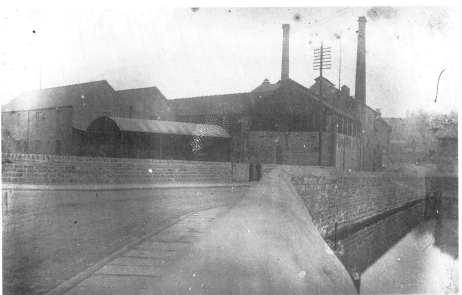

Mansfield Brewery in 1905, this time looking up Littleworth and showing some of the original buildings, before it was rebuilt in 1907. In the right foreground is the River Maun, and the building on the right beyond the river is the Old Ram Inn, since relocated further up Littleworth.

The cooperage, once a feature of every brewery. Today the trade is virtually extinct. Modern barrels are made of aluminium which makes them lighter to handle and more durable. The cooper was a highly skilled craftsman who only qualified after serving a long apprenticeship. It was his job to shape the oak timbers and assemble them to produce a leak-proof barrel.

The cellar, 1905. Here the full barrels were stored awaiting dispatch. Correct storage, usually in a temperature-controlled environment, is vital to maintain the quality of the beer.

The brewery yard as it was in 1905 appears to be rather cramped by today's standards. The barrels standing on their ends on the right are probably waiting to be filled. On the left the back of a rather ancient horse-drawn wagon can be seen.

Brewery transport. One of the brewery's earliest motor lorries. The type is not known, but it is probably a 1920 vintage Morris Commercial. Note the solid tyres and oil lamps. Compare this with today's fleet of bulk tankers and curtain-sided articulated vehicles.

Early transport. This two-horse brewery wagon with its high sides must have required a lot of hard work in loading and unloading. These wagons were replaced by the flat dray type of wagon.

The brewery horse. These gentle giants, usually Shires or Clydesdales, were once a familiar sight around the town as they made the local deliveries. The identity of the gentleman is not known but he was probably the ostler who was responsible for the welfare of the horses.

Rock Valley quarry, above, was one of several limestone quarries in the area which existed in the mid-nineteenth century. Today, only one remains: Gregory's quarry off Nottingham Road. The limestone made a fine building stone as is evident from the older buildings in the town, but as the quarries worked out newer buildings were made of brick. These, such as the phenomenally hard Sherwood brick, were made in the nearby collieries. Most of the disused quarries were used as rubbish dumps and eventually built over, but Rock Valley was used for the buildings and extensions of Barringer, Wallis & Manners Ltd, tin box manufacturers (now CMB Promotional Packaging).

Stone quarrying was once an important industry in the town, employing many men working in several quarries only a mile or so outside the town centre. Before the late nineteenth century, a brick building was a novelty in Mansfield, as this book will confirm. By the time this photograph was taken in 1937 in Quarry Lane, the industry was declining. Now only a small firm in Gregory's quarry on Nottingham Road cuts stone for restoration purposes and for the production of fireplace surrounds.

Red moulding sand from the Berry Hill quarries was awarded a Gold Medal at the Great Exhibition of 1851. Sand was quarried in the eighteenth century and transported by pack mules and wagons. Railways in the next century facilitated distribution world wide until modern technology rendered traditional mould-making methods obsolete. The sand is now dug for building and construction purposes.

Iron and brass founding has a long history in Mansfield, due perhaps to the existence of the fine moulding sand available locally. The picture below is of the entrance to Sanderson's Foundry on Leeming Street, while the foundry yard is shown left. The firm moved from this site to Hermitage Lane in 1903 to make way for the public library and museum. The firm moved again in 1903, to Sheepbridge Lane, and was taken over by the Meadow Foundry in 1957.

Meadow Foundry. Founded in Littleworth by William Richardson, the company was incorporated in 1872 and the founder remained its managing director until his retirement in 1907. He also founded a bullet works on Victoria Street which was taken over by his brother Antonio who also built the Picturedrome cinema on Belvedere Street. The Meadow Foundry moved to Sheepbridge Lane in 1963 to join a subsidiary, Sanderson's, but went out of business in 1985.

Mansfield Colliery was the third coal mine sunk by the Bolsover Colliery Co. By 1925 there were six: Bolsover, sunk 1891; Creswell, sunk 1894; Mansfield, sunk 1905; Rufford, sunk 1913; Clipstone, sunk 1922 (though work had begun prior to the outbreak of the First World War); and Thoresby, sunk 1925 – all following the Top Hard coal seam.

The company, under its managing director John Plowright Houfton, was extremely active locally, building 'model villages' for its workforce (including institutes and drill halls) at its collieries, and instigating the building of the Mansfield Railway which connected the Great Central Railway at Kirkby with that at Clipstone. J.P. Houfton himself became mayor of Mansfield, a high sheriff of Nottinghamshire, an MP for East Nottingham and was knighted the year before his death in 1929.

The firm of Barringer, Wallis & Manners Ltd, tin box manufacturers, was honoured in 1914 with an inspection from King George V and Queen Mary, who were on an official visit to Mansfield. The firm had enjoyed great success since being formally split off from Messrs Barringer & Co., mustard manufacturers, in 1890. It had become a limited company in 1895. In 1897 property was purchased at Oddicroft Mill in Sutton-in-Ashfield, and in 1908 a new building was opened in Rock Valley. Extensions to the Rock Valley buildings were completed in 1927. In 1939 the firm was taken over by the Metal Box Co., while the present concern is a subsidiary of a company formed from a merger of the packaging interests of Metal Box with that of a French firm, Carnaud SA.

The origins of the firm reflect the gradual shift in importance from the manufacture of mustard, to the boxes in which it was contained, and thus the development of tin boxes for all sorts of other products. Among the most successful of these latter were those produced for Jacobs biscuits, which used illustrations from Lewis Carroll's *Through the Looking Glass*. Permission had to be obtained from the author, the Revd C.L. Dodgson, who agreed on condition that he received a hundred or so empty tins for his own use. The firm upset him once, however, when they sent him a box filled with Jacobs biscuits thinking this would please him. It didn't – he sent them back with the complaint that he only wanted empty tins and, in any case, he preferred Huntley & Palmers biscuits!

Faire Brothers factory stood on Burns Street and, as may be seen here, employed more women than men in the production of insoles and heel stiffeners for shoes. The product went through three processes, pressing, moulding and finally glueing, before being packed and dispatched. These photographs from 1949 were loaned by Mrs K. Baugh (née Beal) who worked here.

Councillor Harold Simpson, mayor of Mansfield in 1958–9, accompanied by the mayoress, Mrs Gladys Simpson, paid an official visit to Mansfield Metal Box Co., where he in fact worked as a toolsetter. Here he is inspecting the Extrusion Department, where Mr Howard Dugdale, department head (second from left), accompanied the official party.

Maltings, Midworth Street. Up to the 1850s there were twenty-six malthouses in Mansfield. By around 1930 only the Maltings remained. The Maltings was originally a separate business from Mansfields Brewery but became incorporated soon after one of the Maltings' partners, Addison Titley of Gilcroft House, became a partner in the brewery. It closed in 1974, was sold to the Council in 1978 and became a night-club in 1982.

The Mansfield Shoe Co. started life as Royce, Gascoine & Co. in 1871. By 1891 there was a factory in Leicester as well as in Mansfield. In January 1900 the Mansfield side of the business was formed into a separate company, Mansfield Shoe Co. Ltd, with premises on Dallas Street. In 1907 the company introduced the 'Devonshire' range of women's shoes and in 1935 became a founder member of the Norvic Group of companies. In the 1960s and 1970s there were about 700 people employed at Dallas Street, but by 1981, when the Norvic Group went into receivership, the number had declined to about 350. The Mansfield Shoe Co. (1981) Ltd arose out of the ashes, however, and now employs about 650 people in factories in Mansfield, Harworth and Bristol.

SECTION FOUR

Commerce

Mr J.C. Eadson of Eclipse Yard, Westgate, posing with his prizewinning outfit at the Carters' Show in 1913.

The Co-operative stores as they were from 1922 until the early 1960s, when the frontage was remodelled and the clock tower removed. Since then the premises have been greatly extended and a bridge built across Stockwell Gate to link with other departments.

Mansfield Co-operative Society was formed in 1864, in small premises on Leeming Street, opening evenings only. A year later a store was built on Stockwell Gate, with an adjacent steam flour mill. Enlarged in 1908, this building, shown in the photograph, caught fire in 1918 and was rebuilt and opened in 1922 with improved facilities.

The dividend was an important contribution to household budgets and often gave a return of 2s 6d in the pound. Here, a queue of members waits on Queen Street in 1926 to receive what is due to them. One old lady recalled that her mother usually bought her a new frock with the 'Divi' so that she could look her best on the chapel Whit Walk.

Bennett's saddlery shop on Leeming Street in 1895, when the horse was still a cornerstone of commerce and trade. The proprietor stands in the door, his craftsmen and apprentices lined up in front of the windows which are dressed with items of harness, whips and horse medicines. Collars for heavy horses and blankets are displayed outside.

Pavement traders on Westgate paid smaller market tolls than did stall-holders, although they caused greater inconvenience to pedestrians and annoyed shopkeepers who resented the clutter on their frontages. Here a trader is selling rabbits, no doubt freshly snared. Modern hygiene has banned the sale of meat from the open market.

Mr Robert Greenwood was a sanitary plumber who had been quick to extend his business at No. 67 Westgate, to take advantage of the newly introduced electrical supply in the town. This view of 1904 is very interesting, as the workmen in the foreground were probably involved with the laying down of tram rails in preparation for the service, begun in July of that year. Note the congestion caused by the market traders. By the time the photograph below was taken, during the 1960s, the tram lines had long been removed and the Granada cinema, formerly the Plaza, built on the site of Mr Greenwood's shop. The featured film was *The Magnificent Two* starring Morecambe and Wise.

The Sherwood Photographic Co. had premises on Westgate from 1881 until a fire in 1932. The proprietor, Mr George Ellis, also had studios in Bridge Street and Albert Street, the latter being his only shop after the fire. In this photograph of 1900 the glass-roofed studio can be seen above the shop in which artists' materials were sold. Mr Ellis's daughters Polly and Erika (Bacon) helped in the business. Below, these pedestrians are looking across the road towards Ellis's premises. Note the carrier's cart outside the Nag's Head public house.

Ye Olde Refreshment House, seen here in 1930, was formerly known as Caunt's Café. It stood on the corner of King's Head Yard, Stockwell Gate, and at the time of its demolition in 1972 was revealed to have been a medieval cruck frame structure. It was planned to preserve the oak beams but sadly they were burnt by the demolition team.

The Starbright Stores were an additional business venture of Mr William Hornby, landlord of the Masons' Arms on Leeming Street, next to Blasky's wallpaper store. Beyond was Mr Widdison, tripe dealer. The canopy of the Victoria Hall can be seen in this 1910 photograph.

Mann's bakery stood on the corner of Mount Street and Chesterfield Road South and, as may be seen from this 1910 postcard, was a thriving family business boasting four delivery carts. The proprietor was an important contributor to the 1927 celebration of the 700th anniversary of the Market Charter and the 550th of the July Fair, as he baked the traditional gooseberry pork pie to be ceremonially sliced by Alderman D.H. Maltby, mayor, at a table set up in front of the Town Hall.

The junction of Westgate and the Market Place was a hazardous spot in 1926, to judge from the speed at which these ladies are crossing the road. A few years after, the premises, from Carr's shoe shop on the right to the lower building near the tram, would be demolished during the Clerkson's Alley slum clearance scheme, and Regent Street would be created.

Leckenby's grocers shop on Leeming Street was opened in 1900 as 'Crow and Leckenby'. It was always regarded as a high-class establishment and older residents will remember the fragrance of freshly roasted coffee beans pervading the street. The firm closed in the 1960s.

Leeming Street post office in 1969, at the time that Mr Syd Dernley was sub-postmaster there. A public executioner from 1949 to 1953, he collected memorabilia connected with this and the cellar under the premises contained a gallows from Cambridge Prison. In his retirement, he produced a book of his experiences, entitled *A Hangman's Tale*.

Market stalls have scarcely changed in style since Mr A.S. Buxton took these photographs in 1900. Present-day shoppers would not expect to buy crockery displayed on the ground and would also find the range of flowers rather poor, as there appears to be only marguerites, a few arum lilies and some aspidistra to top the display. Then, as now, the trader has artistically arranged his vegetables and fruit to best effect and no doubt would refuse to disturb them before he had sold the loose stock from hidden boxes.

Mansfield Cattle Market opened on 3 January 1878, bringing to an end the long-established practice of livestock auctions taking place by the old Market Cross in Westgate and, since 1870, in the Market Place. Animals frequently ran amok, even entering premises and tossing passers-by, and by 1874 the Town's Commissioners were seriously considering two sites for a purpose-built market, eventually purchasing a field by the Water Meadows from the Duke of Portland for 2s 6d per yard. Mansfield-born architect Watson Fothergill designed the buildings, only one of which survives near the Water Meadows Wet Leisure Centre which occupies the site. These photographs were taken around the turn of the century.

Mr Frank Daughton of 80 Stockwell Gate and his horse, 'Dolly', made a daily milk round for many years, in the period when milk was ladled from the can into customers' jugs. Here 'Dolly' is anticipating a titbit from the open window of Lawville Bakery at 41 Dallas Street, kept by the Gadd family.

Church and Chapel

Throughout its eight hundred and more years, St Peter's church has not only been the town's principal place of worship but also a focal point for much that has happened in the life of the community.

During the nineteenth century Mansfield's population increased considerably. At that time, when church attendance was much higher than today, St Peter's was too small for such numbers. The decision to build St John's church arose out of this situation. It was completed and dedicated in 1856. The top picture has the look of an architect's sketch while the bottom one shows the church as it was built with its associated school next to it. When this was opened in 1862 Mr Herbert Columbine was in charge of the boys' school and during his first year of office he admitted eighty-eight pupils. At the first inspection, carried out in July 1863, it was reported that 'The boys are in fair order', though it was added that 'The text of the Catechism should be better known.' On 29 September, the anniversary of the opening, the children were given apples to mark the occasion.

Concerned for the spiritual well-being of the men working on the Midland Railway's extension that ran through the town and on to Worksop, the contractor had a mission room built for them on Stockwell Gate (above). This was dedicated in 1870 and familiarly known as the Red Barn. Railway work complete, the building was acquired by St Peter's church as a place of worship for the people in that expanding part of town. Following the creation of St Mark's parish in 1889, it continued to serve the same purpose for the next three years. It was then replaced by a corrugated iron building which in turn was superseded by the present church in 1896 (below). This was designed by the London architect Mr Temple Moore, and built by Fisher Brothers of Mansfield. The stone-laying ceremony was a splendid occasion, performed by the Duke of Portland and watched by more than two thousand people. Meanwhile the Stockwell Gate mission continued to be used as a Sunday school, a purpose it served until 1921 when it closed. The premises were disposed of and subsequently used as a cycle shop.

During the nineteenth century no fewer than four different Methodist denominations maintained places of worship in Mansfield. From humble beginnings, when they met in makeshift rooms, the Primitive Methodists built their first chapel in 1842 in Queen Street. Forty years later it was described as 'cribb'd, cabin'd, confin'd', and was clearly too small. Never a wealthy denomination, it was only after considerable sacrifice that sufficient funds were raised to complete a more spacious chapel. A site was obtained on the corner of Leeming Street with Terrace Road, and on 27 April 1886 the recently elected MP for Mansfield, Mr C.G.S. Foljambe, laid the foundation stone. The day was gloriously warm; some ladies felt it necessary to raise their parasols (above) and the occasion was one of great rejoicing. The chapel (below) remained the head of the Mansfield Primitive Methodist circuit until Methodist union in 1932. Subsequently it formed part of the Nottingham Road circuit until it was closed in the 1960s. More recently it has been re-opened and is used by the followers of the Church of the God of Prophecy.

By the time of his marriage in 1937 to Miss Phyllis Holmes, Mr Christopher Carr had already been a bell-ringer at St Peter's church for ten years. After ringing for the ceremony, the team, joined by the bridegroom (centre back row), posed for this picture. The captain, Mr Herbert Allsop, began ringing in 1884 while his vice-captain, Mr Charles Carr, father of the groom, was also a veteran of Victorian days. As a 17-year-old he had rung for the Queen's Diamond Jubilee celebrations in 1897.

Few ceremonies, either civic or religious, that took place in Mansfield in the early days of the century were regarded as complete without the presence of either the Duke or Duchess of Portland. It was the latter who graced the stone laying of St Lawrence's church which took place at the end of October 1908. Always prominent and easily recognized, being 6ft tall, here she was especially so because of her ostrich plumed hat. The church, which replaced a small and inadequate mission room, was consecrated by the Bishop of Southwell in the following year.

After it had been standing for only six years, faithful members of this Wesleyan Methodist chapel on Stockwell Gate found the doors barred against them as they attempted to enter for Sunday worship. Some of the erstwhile members had defected and had seized the chapel for the newly formed Methodist New Connexion. For that morning the Wesleyans had to hold their service in the open, in the Market Place. In 1815 the chapel, then disused, was bought by the Baptists for £280. It served as their place of worship until 1912 when it was replaced by a new chapel on Rosemary Street. In 1974 both this and its predecessor were demolished to make way for the ring road.

By the 1870s the Wesleyan chapel on Bridge Street was firmly established and well attended. Although its 800 seats would rarely be fully occupied, congregations of around 600 made them seem so. Accordingly, in 1885, a mission room was built in nearby Newgate Lane. Although subsequently enlarged it remained a modest building, drawing much of its support from the smaller, poorer houses of its immediate neighbourhood. By the early 1950s membership had fallen to twelve and it closed in 1958. The premises are now used as a shop selling television sets and electrical goods.

This crowd gathered in 1889 to witness the stone-laying of a Sunday school for the United Methodists. It faced Albert Street and though its frontage has been much altered its appearance remains unchanged at the back.

This sombre-looking chapel was built in 1839 on St John's Street for Mansfield's least known non-conformist church, the Methodist New Connexion. Formed in 1797 when they appropriated the Stockwell Gate chapel of the Wesleyans, their subsequent history is largely unknown. For some years in the middle of the nineteenth century the chapel served as the head of a small single-minister circuit, though by 1870 it had closed and was being used as a warehouse. It is now a furniture store.

The bells of St Peter's church have rung out for centuries, calling the faithful to worship. For seven months, however, in 1948, they were silent, having been removed for recasting at Taylor's foundry at Loughborough. By November of that year the work had been completed and the bells returned. They were placed in the church for rededication before hanging and here this photograph was taken. The vicar, the Revd S.C. Bulley, later to become Bishop of Penrith, is standing centre and he is flanked by the two churchwardens, Mr N.M. Lane and Mr S. Richardson. At the service of rededication, held on Sunday 14 November, Canon R.F. Wilkinson, a former curate of the church, a noted antiquary and authority on campanology, preached the sermon and told the congregation a little about the history of the bells. He informed them that the peal was made up to eight in 1762 which was also the last occasion on which the others had been recast. The largest bell, prominently shown on the picture, still bore its original inscription, 'Two summons by this bell we have, one to the church and one to the grave.' It was dated 1610. To this had been added, 'Re-cast 1948, the third year of the Atomic Age. A day of doubt, men's hearts failing them for fear, thus we ring out that all the voice of God may hear.' An old custom, long in abeyance, was revived a few days after the bells had been rededicated. One Thursday evening the bell-ringers climbed the church tower to take part in the ceremony of 'turning-over' the bells. Having done that, accompanied by the vicar, the churchwardens and the secretary of the Parochial Church Council, they walked across the road to the Eight Bells Hotel, the traditional headquarters of the ringers. Here the landlord served them with bread, cheese and ale and after he had been thanked, the evening was concluded with a short recital on an old set of handbells.

The passion play at St Peter's church was produced by Miss W. Baggaley at Easter 1935. The performers, members of the Youth Fellowship, rehearsed at Grove House, afterwards giving the play at the parish church and St John's church. Mrs Phyllis Carr, right, remembers that the two living doves, which were intended to sit docilely in the basket she carried, were recalcitrant and, during the St John's performance, flew off into the roof of the church. This tableau represented the three Marys.

SECTION SIX

Health and Welfare

The Princess Royal, Countess of Harewood, inspected Red Cross nurses and visited Mansfield General Hospital on 27 April 1944. She was escorted by Mr John Harrop White.

Mansfield General Hospital stone-laying. In 1889, due mainly to the efforts of Mr D.J. Patterson and his committee, a site for the new hospital was purchased on West Hill Drive. On 11 November 1889 the foundation stone was laid by Mrs Hollins of Pleasley Vale.

The opening ceremony was carried out by his Grace the Duke of Portland on 27 October 1890. The hospital, which had cost £2,000 to build, provided accommodation for five beds, one of which was endowed by the Duchess of Portland.

The Mansfield Hospital Jubilee Extension, 1897. The foundation stone was laid on 28 June 1897 by Mr F.W. Webb of Newstead, the president of the hospital board. Also present were the mayor and mayoress, Alderman and Miss Barringer, Canon Pavey and Mr Hollins, the chairman of the hospital board.

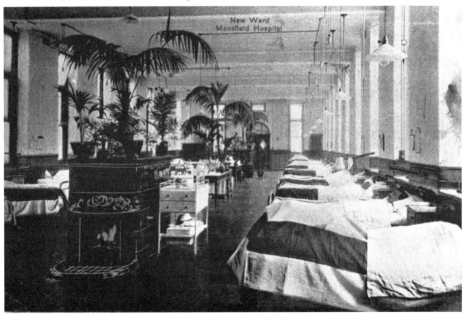

The interior of the new extension. On completion, the new wing was named the Newstead ward. Said to have been of modern design, with heating by central stove, it provided accommodation for a further ten beds, bringing the total for the hospital at the time to fifteen.

The Ransom Sanatorium on Ratcher Hill, opened in 1902 at a time when tuberculosis was rampant. Its open-plan wards were designed to give the patients maximum fresh air, a vital part of their treatment. In recent years it served for a time as a psychiatric unit until mining subsidence forced its closure.

The Forest Hospital for infectious diseases, once known locally as the fever hospital, opened in 1893. Initially its two wards were corrugated iron structures, lit by oil lamps. Accommodation was available for twenty-three beds and in 1899 the first fever-trained matron was appointed. In 1915 the foundation stone for a nurses home and administrative block was laid by the mayor, Alderman D.H. Maltby.

The Harlow Wood Orthopaedic Hospital received a visit from the Minister of Health, the Rt Hon. Enoch Powell on 21 June 1962. Here he is being shown around the remedial gymnasium by the physiotherapist, Mr Fred Smart.

Many of the patients were miners, and to help in their rehabilitation a mock-up of a drift mine was introduced, complete with rails and a truck.

Brunts Charity Office and Statue on Leeming Street. Samuel Brunts died in September 1711. Under the terms of his will the sum of £4 was to be distributed annually to needy persons over the age of 60 who had not received alms from any public fund.

The trustees of Brunts Charity in 1894. Front row, from the left: Canon Pavey of St Peter's, -?-, Alderman Robert Barringer, the mayor of Mansfield, Alderman G. Pickard, Alderman D. Patterson. On the back row: Alderman G.H. Hibbert, the first mayor of Mansfield in 1891/2, -?-, -?-, -?-, -?-, Alderman J.H. Blake.

Education

Miss Hardwick's school on Clerkson Street was one of many private schools in the town. In this 1895 photograph, the pupils have donned their best clothes for the occasion. The school closed in 1923.

Maltby's Academy juniors line up with well-polished boots, smoothly brushed hair and very respectable clothing for this photograph of 1880, outside the old school building in Rock Court. On the left is Mrs Maltby, wife of John Maltby and mother of fifteen children, of whom one stands on the right. It is unusual to see only one girl wearing a pinafore in a school group of this period. Only the boys continued as seniors.

Miss Susannah Parsons, assisted by her sister, Jane, conducted a school at Westgate House from the 1830s until her death in 1877, caused by fever contracted from polluted well water. Children from Mansfield's foremost families were educated under the guidance of Miss Parsons, whose disciplinary methods were firm and no doubt effective, ranging from the culprit being stood on a stool, to receiving a sharp crack on the head with a wooden pencil box. Another sister, Miss Dorothy, was housekeeper to the Hallowes family at Glapwell Hall. A Carte-de-Visite of 1862.

Miss Macrae surrounded by the school leavers of 1908 outside Queen Elizabeth's Girls' Grammar School. Back row: Maud Haydon, Nellie Taylor, Katie Booth, Olive Plumbe. Second Row: Mary Holliday, Gertrude Westwick, Jessie Doig, Ethel Edge, Winnie Dickson, Olive Fermstone, H. Massey, H. Turner. Third Row: Emily ?, Mary Jamieson, Miss Hackforth, Miss Macrae, Norah Kitchener, Ethel Hodgson. Front row: Sybil Hedderley, Agnes Houfton, Ruth Hedderley, Jessie Tolley, Elsie Nuttall.

The Cricket Club at Mansfield Grammar School in 1898. Back row: Mr Major, Mr H. Walkerdine, Mr Woods, C.C. Plumbe, Mr Young, F.W. Stokes, J.D. Lawton. Second row: B. Priestman, G.S. Warner, H.C. Harrison, R. Tyler (captain), J. Dodsley, J.W. Butterworth. Front row: J. Piggford, C. Chambers.

Ravensdale Council School was opened in 1933 to accommodate senior pupils living on the surrounding estate. It was a model school, built to the best standards of the period. Here, the school hall also serves as a gymnasium. Pupils at council schools were given a day's holiday and prizes if their school achieved at least 92 per cent attendance in one month.

Ravensdale School was opened in 1933 primarily for children of senior age living on the council housing estate which, since the mid-1920s, had spread over an area of 98 acres previously owned by the Duke of Portland and used for farming. Here headteacher Mr Edwin Ely, in the centre of the front row, is photographed with his staff of those early days. Mr Ely came from Pleasley, was educated at The Brunts School and Leeds University and died in office in 1954. His deputy, Miss Dorothy Weddle, seated on his right, later became headteacher of High Oakham School.

Miss Oldhouse's reception class at King Edward's Infants School in 1937, learning through play activity in accordance with advanced educational principles of the period. In the photograph are Sheila Jelly, John Glover, Betty North, Eric (Titch) Green and on the right Rhoda White (Cope) who supplied the photograph.

King Edward's Council School pupils proudly displaying their individual certificates won for solo singing and recitation at the 1938 Music and Drama Festival, held at High Oakham School. The large cup was awarded for choral singing and was filled with lemonade for the children to drink. Left is Mr Mark Widdowson, and right Miss Ada Clarke. Dorothy Pothecary, who loaned the photograph, stands next to Miss Clarke.

Queen Elizabeth's Boys' Grammar School, 1928. The opening of the memorial pavilion took place on 9 September 1928. The ceremony was performed by Field Marshal Viscount Allenby, assisted by his aide-de-campe, Lieutenant C.A. Smith. Also present was the mayor, Alderman Joseph Beck, the headmaster, Mr L. Burgess, and Mr J. Harrop White, the chairman of the governors.

Field Marshal Viscount Montgomery of Alamein visited Queen Elizabeth's Boys' Grammar School on 13 July 1949. He inscribed, and formally deposited in the school library, the Service Record Book of Old Elizabethans who had fought with him in the desert and Normandy. Advising the assembled pupils that character kept a man straight and earned him respect, he emphasized that modern youth should visit the barber more often.

A civic welcome at the Parochial Hall was held for eighty Danish schoolchildren who visited Mansfield in July 1935, a year after pupils from the Brunts' and Queen Elizabeth's schools had visited Denmark. The mayoress, Mrs E.W. Mellors, deputized for her husband who had been knocked down by a cyclist and badly injured. Mrs Mellors is seen here shaking hands with Miss Jorgenson.

Mansfield School of Art had moved five times since its inauguration at the Mechanics Institute in 1870. On 19 November 1930 the door of a permanent base was unlocked at Ashfield House, behind the recently built Technical College on Chesterfield Road. In the group are Mr J.H. White, chairman of the Art School governors, and Mr Albert Sorby Buxton.

Mr Augustus Savage (left) and Mr Jesse Moore were two of the town's schoolmasters, the former at St Peter's, the latter at St John's. Mr Savage was a hard man, a firm believer in the adage that to spare the rod would inevitably spoil the child, and grown men were known to blanch at his name. One former pupil, returning to Mansfield after more than forty years' residence in Australia, on being asked his most vivid boyhood memory, replied, 'Mr Savage'. Mr Moore, though firm and not averse to corporal punishment when occasion demanded it, was more gentle in manner. On his retirement in 1913, after almost forty-five years in office, it was calculated that at least 4,600 children had passed through his hands and that seventy teachers had served under him. In recognition of his work over so long a time he was presented with an armchair and a purse of gold and it was recorded that Mr Moore carried with him into his retirement the good wishes of all who knew him and many hopes were expressed that he would live long to enjoy his well-earned rest. This photograph, when the two headmasters posed together, was taken around 1890.

Queen Elizabeth's Boys' Grammar School was founded in 1561. It moved to this site on Chesterfield Road in 1878, in buildings shown in the foreground of this aerial view. In the 1970s it became an upper school, taking pupils of all abilities aged 14–18 years. In 1993 the boys' and girls' schools united to become a mixed upper school.

St Lawrence's School was built in 1887 to accommodate the burgeoning child population of the Newgate Lane area. In addition to providing education for 200 pupils aged 5–10 years, the building was consecrated for use as a church, a purpose it fulfilled until St Lawrence's church was built in 1909. At the time of this photograph the setting was rural.

Newgate Lane Council School was built in 1905 to serve an area which was rapidly expanding, the old St Lawrence's School being totally inadequate. A class of more than fifty was not uncommon and no doubt the headmaster, Mr Millott (right), had to use the cane to maintain discipline among the lads, some of whom do appear to have been rather tough nuts. Note the black eye in the second row.

Prefects at Queen Elizabeth's Boys' Grammar School pose with the headmaster, Mr Leslie Brettle, for a group photograph in 1950. It was customary for prefects to wear Oxford undergraduate gowns, awarded at a ceremony in front of the assembled pupils.

SECTION EIGHT
Transport

No doubt hoping to cut a dash as he rode through the town, this unknown Mansfield motorcyclist proudly posed with his machine during the autumn of 1917. Despite many changes in ways of transport, motorcycles have always remained popular. During the inter-war years, with a side car attached, they were the means of many happy family outings.

Many a horse had a hard time of it in turn-of-the-century Mansfield, and the one between the shafts in this picture certainly had to struggle to make progress along the snow-covered winter streets of 1908. It is just passing the end of West Hill Drive and is heading into town. Clearly the inclement weather had kept most people indoors though, for those out and about, the exposed lines show that the trams were still running.

Carriers' carts were a vital part of communications in the past, carrying goods to and from outlying settlements. Forty-eight carriers, starting from inns, are listed in the 1894 Directory, working every weekday except Tuesday. This cart, photographed around 1900, is passing along Bridge Street, to face a steep pull up Ratcliffe Gate.

A travelling family on Berry Hill Lane in 1961, when this now busy stretch of road still retained the grass verges and tranquillity of a country lane marking the southern edge of Mansfield. The family usually set up camp on what is now Chatsworth Drive, then green pasture land belonging to the Firs Farm. Wagons of this type are now collectors' items, but in the past whole families lived their entire lives in similar homes.

Mowing the lawn at Grove House, Brunt Street, around the turn of the century. The horse wears leather hoof-covers to prevent damage to the grass. The combined weight of the machine and the seated gardener must have been considerable. In the border behind the horse, fruit canes are protected by netting.

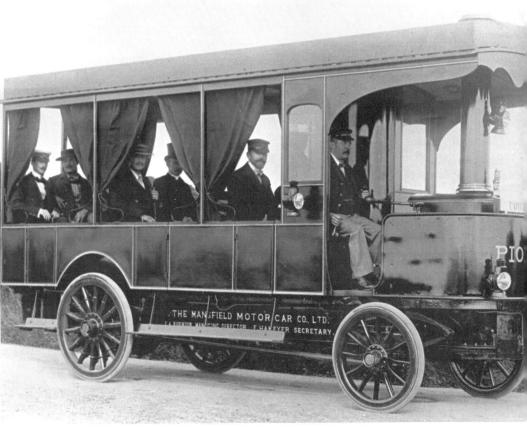

The 'Pioneer' steam omnibus setting out from Cowes, Isle of Wight, on its journey to Mansfield, where it arrived on 30 June 1898. Built for the sum of £600 by the Liquid Fuel Engineering Co. of East Cowes, on behalf of Mansfield Motor Car Co. Ltd, the 'Pioneer' was the first attempt at motorized public transport in Mansfield. Powered by an oil-filled boiler, the 'Pioneer' was capable of carrying twenty-two passengers, with a similar number in a detachable trailing car. It was of a unique design and destined to remain so. The Mansfield Motor Car Co. Ltd was created by some of the leading Mansfield businessmen in the town with the object of maintaining the trade of Mansfield by allowing ease of transport to and from the surrounding towns and villages. The chairman was William J. Chadburn of the Mansfield Brewery, the managing director was Frederick A. Robinson of the ironfounders, Sanderman & Robinson, while one of the other directors was Charles Manners of Barringer, Wallis and Manners, tin box manufacturers. At first it seemed as if the 'Pioneer' would be a success. The journey from Cowes was virtually without incident save for a problem with the solid rubber tyres, as was the first week of commercial operation running between Mansfield, Mansfield Woodhouse, Warsop, Sutton and Hucknall Huthwaite. The problem with the tyres got worse. The solid rubber tyres kept coming off the wheels. Leather straps had to be used to keep them on but these made the whole machine vibrate and they didn't last very long. Unfortunately the problem proved insoluble, and after an intermittent service lasting barely two months, the 'Pioneer' was withdrawn from service.

Town Council outing, 1895. The coach and horses were loaned by Mr J.C. Ringham of the Swan Hotel on Church Street, who used to hire them out for trips to the Dukeries.

Mansfield & District Light Railway Co. Ltd. The tram depot on Sutton Road is shown above, while below is one of the double-decker trams. The trams operated between 1905 and 1932 and carried over 134 million passengers. Radiating out from the Market Place there were five routes: to Mansfield Woodhouse; to Crown Farm (from 1911); to High Oakham; to Huthwaite via Sutton; and to Pleasley.

Before the present Market Place was cleared of the clutter of ancient buildings that filled much of its space, the narrow, alley-like way that led into it from Nottingham Road was called Spittlehouse Gate. Once the market was established, its name was changed to the more appropriate, though less evocative, Market Street. Most of the buildings on the picture, which was taken around 1910, date from the last quarter of the nineteenth century. Clearly the schoolboys had little respect for the starting speed of the tram car.

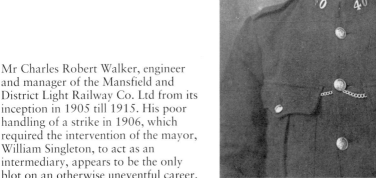

Mr Charles Robert Walker, engineer and manager of the Mansfield and District Light Railway Co. Ltd from its inception in 1905 till 1915. His poor handling of a strike in 1906, which required the intervention of the mayor, William Singleton, to act as an intermediary, appears to be the only blot on an otherwise uneventful career.

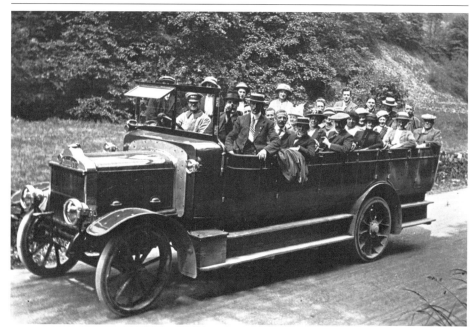

Charabanc outing. Once connected to the railway system and thus easily accessible, Mansfield became a centre of tourism for visitors wishing to see the Dukeries and Sherwood Forest. Charabanc outings were arranged for morning and afternoon trips, leaving and returning to the main hotels in the town, such as the Midland, the Swan and the White Hart.

Underwood's bus turning at the end of Westgate, around 1926. W.T. Underwood began his bus service company in Clowne in 1920 and in the early years the service to Mansfield was from Eckington via Clowne and Bolsover. The company grew, buying out other bus companies, until in 1927 its name was changed to East Midlands Motor Services. W.T. Underwood himself left the company at this time and started up other bus companies.

The car in the photograph is the De Dion, owned by Mr William Jackson Chadburn and kept at Nettleworth Manor. Although there is no written evidence to confirm the names of the two boys enjoying the experience of 'driving' the car, it is quite possible they were Mr Chadburn's two sons, Francis Ludlow, the elder, and Claude William. The photograph is from the Mansfield Brewery Archives.

Car trials at Clipstone. The Duke's Drive at Clipstone was a long, straight, private road which was a popular venue for car trials in the early years of this century. One such was the Gordon Bennett race, sponsored by and named after the proprietor of the *New York Herald* who lived from 1841 to 1918. In 1903 the Honourable Charles S. Rolls made an attempt on the motor speed record at Clipstone.

Mansfield Market Place in the 1920s. Despite the three vehicles visible in this photograph, road traffic does not appear to trouble the thoughts of the family group in the foreground, chatting happily in the middle of the road, nor indeed the photographer either. This was, after all, the main road at the time; the A60 went from Nottingham Road, down Market Street, across the Market Place and up Leeming Street. The conductor is shepherding his passengers on to a tram bound for Mansfield Woodhouse, while waiting patiently to get past the parked car is a lorry belonging to the firm of Barringer, Wallis & Manners, tin box manufacturers, which was to be taken over by Metal Box in 1939.

Mansfield's railway story has not been a happy one. Although steam trains began running into the town in 1849 and although it once possessed two stations, it never stood on a main line and long-distance travel usually involved changing trains and slow journeys. First on the scene was the Midland Railway, which at first ran services between the town and Nottingham until the line was extended to Worksop in 1875. Its station (top) was large and covered with an overall roof which kept the elements out though, unfortunately, the smoke and soot in. This made it a dark and gloomy building, an impression that must have been very apparent at the turn of the century when it was said that more trains passed through it in a day than used St Pancras station in London. It was closed to passenger traffic in 1964. Mansfield's second station was that of the Great Central Railway (below), built in 1916. It stood above the surrounding buildings and was cold and windswept in winter. For a brief spell it ran a direct service to Marylebone in London but for most of its time elderly locomotives with dingy, out-dated carriages chugged to and from Nottingham. It was closed in the mid-1950s.

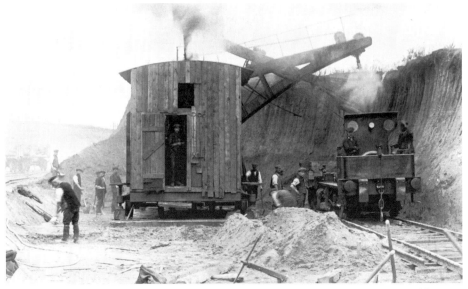

Construction of the Mansfield railway, 1913. The Midland Railway had opened lines to Mansfield in the 1850s, but had successfully rebuffed attempts by other railway companies to open lines in the area. This monopoly was not to the pleasing of the local colliery companies, however, and they determined to do something about it. Accordingly, in 1910, the Mansfield Railway Co. was incorporated, its seven directors including Emerson Bainbridge and John Plowright Houfton, of the Bolsover Colliery Co., and William Jackson Chadburn, of Mansfield Brewery. The line was to be in three parts: from the Great Central Railway near Lindby's Lane, Kirkby to Mansfield; from Mansfield to Mansfield Colliery; and from Mansfield Colliery to the Great Central Railway near Clipstone. The Great Central Railway agreed to work the line.

Construction of the railway took from 1911 to 1916, the first sections to be opened for mineral traffic being from Mansfield Colliery to Clipstone in 1913; the line from Mansfield Colliery to Mansfield was opened in 1914 and the remaining part was finished in 1916. The line was not built purely with mineral traffic in mind. Stations were built at Sutton, Kirkby and Mansfield, and the first passenger train left Nottingham at 7.30 a.m. on 2 April 1917. It arrived in Mansfield at 8.15 a.m. and continued on to Edwinstowe and Ollerton. The line remained in use for passenger traffic until 1956, for mineral traffic a little longer, and the line was taken up a few years later. Today little remains to show for all the work illustrated in these photographs; bridges have been demolished and culverts filled in; the route through the town is now a public footpath called the 'Mansfield Way'.

The *Empress*, a steam locomotive which worked the line at the Bottle Lane/Berry Hill Road sand quarry (driver Mr Cooper). Housewives on Bottle Lane regularly complained about smuts from the engine which dirtied their washing on clothes lines.

The 'Flying Scotsman', 2 September 1971. A red-letter day for local train spotters who turned out in force armed with their cameras to see the 'Flying Scotsman'. They had an added bonus when it stopped at the Midland station to take on water.

With a little ingenuity, local schoolmaster Mr J.T. Burton is able to give his small son a ride on his own version of 'a bicycle made for two'. After teaching for a while in Mansfield, Mr Burton moved to Nottingham before being appointed to headships at Fleckney and Oadby in Leicestershire. His son, Geoffrey, served as a radio operator on Catalina flying boats during the war and died shortly afterwards.

Mounting an 'Ordinary bicycle' was not easy, but this type of mettlesome steed appealed to young bloods who relished the high speeds achieved on a racing machine with a 62 in front wheel. This unknown Mansfield man, dressed in the Victorian equivalent of racing leathers, was possibly mounted on a machine made by Stephen Simpson of Bridge Street. He may have belonged to the Sherwood Forest Bicycle Club which had its headquarters at the Eclipse Inn on the Market Place. Solitary cyclists in the town had to watch out for urchins whose favourite 'sport' was to thrust a stick through the spokes, with disastrous results.

Welbeck Abbey was the destination, on 4 October 1921, for 700 children who had lost their fathers in the First World War. Transport from Mansfield Market Place was by charabanc, car or motorcycle and, in spite of inclement weather, the Duke and Duchess of Portland ensured that the children could enjoy their games and tea under cover in the great Riding School. Every child was given a penny and a bag of sweets before setting back home.

Mrs Kate Ringham, wife of John Charles Ringham, landlord of the Swan Hotel, is seen here in 1905 with her maid Kate Parsons, who married Bill Edge, the hotel's coachman. Mrs Ringham was a vivacious character who worked extensively for charitable causes. In 1910 the hotel yard in which this photograph was taken was glassed over and closed by doors at each end.

SECTION NINE

Leisure

The Old Mansfield Society visited Thurgarton Priory, 22 June 1921. Here the committee members and their hosts, Mr and Mrs Holmes Reddan, pose on the old coach from the Swan Hotel.

Mansfield Swimming Club was founded in 1907 and by 1913, when this photograph of the crack water polo team was taken, had about 160 members. The club's headquarters were at the Mechanics Institute on Queen Street and club night was Thursday. Committee meetings took place in a room at the swimming baths.

The public baths on Bath Street was Mansfield's first 'civic' building, erected in 1853 by the Vestry of Mansfield, designed by Charles Neale who laid out the cemetery grounds, and built by Charles Lindley with stone from his Chesterfield Road quarry on a site given by the Duke of Portland. Water was drawn from wells in the garden at the rear and heating in the early years was by means of waste heat from the adjacent Maun Foundry. The extension on the right was built in 1904 and contained a large swimming pool.

The Central Baths, seen here in 1961, appear very small in comparison with the new Water Meadows Wet Leisure Centre. This pool was constructed in 1904 when extensions were made to the 1853 building. Subsidence, due to coal mining, became an increasing problem here and the whole building was demolished in 1990.

The donkeys of William Sills, seen here at the top of White Hart Street in 1900, have a lighter load to look forward to than normal on this day. Their usual work was the transportation of quarry stone, but a break of a sort took place during the July Fair, when the only weight they were obliged to carry was that of children and others who wished to take advantage of the donkey rides around the town.

Picturedrome cinema, Belvedere Street. Built as a silent movie theatre in 1920, it ceased to operate as a full-time cinema in 1924, became the Queen's theatre from 1934 to 1938, and was a British Restaurant from 1941 to 1950.

Granada cinema, Westgate. Opened in 1930 as the Plaza, its name was changed to the Granada in 1947. It was the largest cinema in the town with seating for over 1,500 and both the cinema and its restaurant are still remembered by many. During the 1960s, to combat falling attendance, live concerts were introduced, including the Beatles (as a supporting act to Helen Shapiro), Billy Fury and Cliff Richard. It was demolished in 1973.

Mr William Daws (above), first curator of Mansfield Museum. The museum was bequeathed to the town by Mr W.E. Baily, majority shareholder of the Mansfield Brewery. Following Baily's death in 1904, the corrugated iron museum and its contents were transported from Penzance (where Baily had lived) to Mansfield. William Daws died in 1930 and in 1932 the old museum was demolished to make way for the present one.

The 8th Sherwood Foresters concert party, 1919. The concert party was formed in France in 1918. Its organizer was 2nd Lt William Pennington of Worksop, assisted by Sgt Parkinson. The comedian of the party, described as screamingly funny, was Private Radford of Mansfield, who was the former stage manager of the Empire theatre, Mansfield.

Mansfield Amateur Operatic Society performed *HMS Pinafore* at the Victoria Hall in April 1911, their sixth production since the Society was founded. Nearly fifty members took part on a very cramped stage, with Mr Harry Walkerdine taking the lead part of Sir Joseph Porter. Proceeds were donated to local charities.

Harry Walkerdine was a native of Nottingham who became editor and manager of the *Mansfield Reporter*. A man of many talents, he played every position in the forward line for Notts County in the 1880s and 1890s, was captain of Mansfield Cricket Club, president of the Bowling Club and the Harriers, and he taught part-time at the grammar school. He was the leading comedian in the Mansfield Amateur Operatic Society and this photograph shows him in *HMS Pinafore*.

Miss Ethel Housely was one of three sisters prominent in educational and musical circles in the town. She progressed from supporting roles in the Amateur Operatic Society to principal parts, including that of Queen Elizabeth in *Merrie England* in 1926. Miss Ethel and Miss Nellie taught music in their home on Leyton Avenue. Miss Gladys, the longest lived, was a school-teacher.

The brass band is often associated with either a works or a colliery and as the number of local mines increased during the second half of the nineteenth century and encroached closer to Mansfield so the unique sound of their bands became an integral part of the town's musical life. Sinking began at Crown Farm in 1904 and coal was raised two years later. A new village, Forest Town, was built to provide accommodation and amenities for the miners and their families. Following the usual pattern, a band was formed and soon developed the proficiency to lead processions, give concerts and take part in contests. That it was successful in the latter is clear from the inclusion of the word 'prize' in its name and the display of the three trophies (above). Here the band is posed by the side of the Welfare Hall, built by the Bolsover Colliery Co., and, judging by the cups and medals on show, the quartet below were just as adept at winning as the full band. Times change and, although brass band music is still popular in the town, the only resident band now is that of the Salvation Army.

Mansfield Amateur Orchestra photographed in 1900 outside the music shop on Dame Flogan Street, which was kept by Mr Henry Carlin, conductor of the orchestra. Their repertoire was extensive, pieces being selected from thirty-seven possible items to be performed at garden parties, flower shows, fêtes and balls. Carlin's shop kept a wide range of sheet music until it closed in recent years.

Mansfield and District Music Club, 1 October 1946, on the occasion of the Civic Opening of the new Parochial Hall on Brunts Street, adjacent to Grove House. Lord Morven Cavendish-Bentinck, younger son of the Duke of Portland, presided at the ceremony and presented a Bechstein grand piano for use at the club recitals. Clothing was still very 'utility' in appearance.

A pageant to celebrate the golden wedding of the Duke and Duchess of Portland was performed in July and August 1939. Mansfield's episode represented the state visit of Charles I and Henrietta Maria to Welbeck in 1642. Mrs Adele Roscoe arranged a ballet and Mrs J.D. Gregory produced the play. Leading parts were taken by Mr R. Bacon, Mrs Gustav Reddan, Mr S. Richardson and Mrs J. Windsor.

Mansfield has never been averse to dressing up when occasion has presented itself and here some of its townspeople are clad in eighteenth-century costume. They are taking part in an Old English Fayre which was part of the Mayor's Hospital Carnival Week of 1927. Standing centre and facing the camera is Mr Albert Sorby Buxton, artist and antiquary, headmaster of the Mansfield School of Art and joint founder of the Old Mansfield Society. He was deeply interested in the town of his birth, writing of its history and painting scenes of its bygone appearance. Fortunately, many of these are now on show in the museum.

Mansfield Society of Artists was founded in 1934 and, apart from the war years, has since then held an annual exhibition at the Art Gallery, Leeming Street. This photograph was taken in 1970 and shows, left to right, Mr Hector McDonald Sutton (principal of Mansfield School of Art and president of the Society of Artists), Mrs Honor Redman (secretary of the Society), Alderman T.S. Martin (mayor of Mansfield and artist), and Mrs Martin (mayoress).

A hockey team made up of prefects from the boys' and girls' grammar schools in 1905, a photograph which illustrates how restricting the girls' clothing must have been. Some parents disapproved of hockey, regarding it as an unladylike game.

Mansfield Lawn Tennis Club was founded in 1888 and a year later had sixty-four members who played on four grass courts near Pheasant Hill. Twenty years later the number of courts was increased to nine, and two hard courts were added. In the 1930s facilities were improved by the erection of a club house and pavilion and a badminton group was formed. This photograph was taken in the mid-1890s.

Mansfield Town Council cricket team, photographed at the Stanhope Street ground on 26 July 1899. Included in this group of leading citizens of the town are, standing left to right: John Harrop White (town clerk), Alderman J.E. Birks, R. Langley (rate collector), W.F. Sanders (mayor), A.H. Limb (town clerk's assistant), W. Jolley, Horace Mettham, J. Skidmore (town crier), and Lodge Richmond (umpire). Front row: H. Campbell (gas and water collector), Alderman J.H. Blake, Councillor D.H. Maltby, Councillor J.G. Ager, Mr A. Graham (gas and water manager), Councillor P.J. Shacklock.

A popular summer outing for Mansfield folk at the turn of the century was by horse-drawn brake to the arboreal delights of Sherwood Forest and the splendours of the Dukeries. The brake was the predecessor of the motorized charabanc and held up to two dozen people seated crosswise. It was drawn by two or four horses, depending on the load and the nature of the journey. The young man in the foreground appears to be carrying a cricket bag so the vehicle he is about to board may have been taking a local team to an away fixture. Cricket has always been popular in Mansfield and at the time of the picture the town club was able to field a number of teams each week during the season.

Mansfield Town Football Club came into being in 1910. Previously several clubs in the town had vied for local support. Prominent among them were Mansfield Greenhalgh, the work's team of Greenhalgh's mill, Mansfield Mechanics and Mansfield Wesley. It was the latter that changed its name to Mansfield Town, thus forming the town club. Until the 1931 season, when they were elected to the Football League, the 'Stags' played in various minor leagues. Since then their fortunes have varied, though from time to time notable achievements have thrilled the Field Mill crowd.

St Mark's football team, 1901/2, one of a number of church teams in Mansfield in the early part of the century. They are, on the back row from the left: A. Ball (trainer), J. Clark, A. Goddard, E.A. Thrall (secretary), P. Maltby, A. Anderson, A. Hodgkinson, G. Kirk. Centre: W. Marriot, W. Marvell, G. Richardson (captain), F. Bryan, A. Smith. At the front: R. Banister, P. Pothecary, F. Ward.

Mansfield Bowling Club, 1900. This is the oldest bowling club in the district. The exact date of its origin is uncertain, but it certainly goes back to the eighteenth century. The headquarters of the club is the Bowl in Hand on Leeming Street and the green, the oldest in Mansfield, is at the rear of the inn.

The Racecourse Recreation Ground, opened on 30 March 1931, offers a range of outdoor sporting activities. In the last century it was a popular racecourse with horse races sponsored by the Duke of Portland and the Duke of Newcastle. Mansfield had three training establishments at this time, the largest being at Sherwood Hall. The last race at Mansfield took place in 1874.

Mansfield Rugby League Club was formed in 1948 by a group of enthusiasts. Their home ground was at the Rainworth Miners' Welfare, and their first match was a friendly against Dewsbury. In 1984 the town had its own team of professionals, the Mansfield Marksmen, sponsored by the Mansfield Brewery. Sadly the club has now disbanded.

Mansfield Colliery's first sports day was held on the Forest Town Welfare cricket ground on 12 June 1909. It was said to have attracted a good entry for both the foot and cycle events. Here one of the cycle races is about to start. The president for the day was Mr J.P. Houfton, the general manager of the Bolsover Co.

The Rufford Hunt assembling in Mansfield's Market Place prior to moving off for the chase. It would need a vivid imagination to picture a scene like this today, but it did happen in 1902. At that time the open countryside would have been only a few minutes' ride from the town centre in any direction.

Ingoldmells was the destination of needy children at Whitsun 1937, when St Peter's Youth Fellowship organized an outing and picnic to this popular east coast resort, much frequented by Mansfield holidaymakers. Photograph by Mr Chris Carr.

Employees of Faire Brothers posed for a group photograph before climbing into single-decker buses for the annual works outing in 1949.

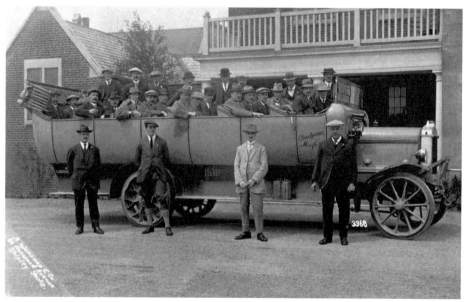

Forest Town Miners Welfare, a centre for the social life of the village for many years, where miners could relax in the evenings with their wives and friends. This party of miners is about to set off for a day's outing, probably to the races, in their 1920 vintage luxury charabanc.

More redolent of a holiday brochure, this photograph of King's Mill reservoir was taken before its waters were infested with unsightly algae and regarded as unsuitable for recreational use. It was constructed in the 1830s to provide a sufficient head of water for the 4th Duke of Portland's extensive irrigation scheme known locally as the Flood Dykes. The name King's Mill refers to the legend which tells how John Cockle, a miller in these parts, once gave shelter to the King, John or Henry II (accounts vary), who had separated from his hunting party and was lost in the forest. The grateful king knighted the hospitable miller, an incident commemorated by the present-day hostelry, the Sir John Cockle. Robert Dodsley, born in Mansfield, dramatist and bookseller in eighteenth-century London, also perpetuated the story in his play, *The King and the Miller of Mansfield*. This was successful in its time though rarely performed now. It was last seen in the town around 1980 in a production by the Queen Elizabeth Grammar Schools. The last King's Mill, supposed successor to John Cockle's more humble dwelling and work place, was destroyed by fire in 1963. Meanwhile, the reservoir had become a popular leisure-time amenity. It was skated on in due season, local anglers tried their luck from its banks and a sailing club criss-crossed its placid surface. Perhaps its oddest use occurred annually in the 1890s when, on Life-Boat day, a life-boat, brought into town for the occasion, was launched into it. The life-boat carried out simulated rescues and was the focus of aquatic sports and games. In the background (right) is the distinctive shape of Hamilton Hill, a prominent feature of the landscape of unknown origin, antiquity or purpose.

St Peter's Boy Scouts, 1923, posing in front of the former Grove House on Midworth Street, then the St Peter's parish hall. The scout masters are: left, Mr J. Allsop, centre, Revd Woodcock, and right, Dr Hunnard. The boy sitting at centre front is Bernard Eastgate.

August is often an uncertain month for weather and these Mansfield boy scouts certainly found it to be so in 1911 while they were in camp at Windsor. No fewer than three thunderstorms blackened the sky and dampened their activities. The high spot of their week under canvas was a visit from Lord Roberts, one of Britain's victorious generals of the Boer War. Although quite smart, a little variety in turn-out was clearly permitted as the boy on the extreme left is wearing a kilt.

SECTION TEN

Inns

The Old Blue Boar, Stockwell Gate, in 1880. Rebuilt in 1888, it was closed in July 1988 and then redeveloped into offices. The 1888 façade was retained.

The Waggon and Coals Inn, Ratcliffe Gate, dates back to a period when Mansfield was better known for the production of malt than of coal. There were said to be some thirty malt kilns in the town in the eighteenth century. Coal had to be brought into the town from Teversal and Blackwell to a coal yard near to the inn, where the maltsters paid from 4d to 6d a hundredweight for it. In common with many early inns, the Waggon brewed its own beer, and produced its own malt. A corner of the old malt kiln can be seen in the lower right hand corner of the picture. The large building in the background is the former Bradley's cotton doubling mill. The Waggon and Coals was demolished in September 1970 to make way for the ring road.

The Eclipse Hotel stood at the corner of the Market and Church Street. It was once a posting inn with coaches leaving for Nottingham at 8 a.m. every weekday. For many years it was the venue for the ancient Swainmote Dinner which was held annually on Holyrood day. This was the day that the Forest Officers of the Crown assembled at a point near Harlow Wood to make their reports, and to receive the charges of the Lord Chief Justice in Eyre. They then adjourned to the Eclipse for an evening of feasting. The last of these functions to take place at the Eclipse was in 1823, after which it was held at the Swan Hotel. The tall building seen on the left of the picture was the third bay of the Swan Hotel. This, along with the Eclipse, was demolished in 1910 to make way for the former National Westminster bank.

The Bulls Head Inn, Portland Street, formerly Bulls Head Lane, a name taken from a former coaching inn which stood near to the site of the present Early Doors. The Bulls Head was built in 1909. It was a popular inn serving a district which was once populated mainly by railway workers. It was demolished in 1972, another victim of the ring road.

The Belle Vue Inn, Stockwell Gate, was built in 1880 and was owned by the former Shipstones Brewery Co. It was demolished shortly after the Bulls Head, again for the ring road. The landlord and landlady at the time of its closure was Mr and Mrs R. Alvey.

The Victoria Hotel, Albert Street, formerly the Cockpit. Cockfighting took place here in the eighteenth century. The pit was at the rear of the hotel on a site once known as Dobbs Croft, now occupied by the Labour Club. During that period it was named the Cock Inn, but later became the Top White Bear. It was purchased by the Mansfield Brewery Co. in 1878.

The Old White Bear Inn once occupied a site at the corner of Albert Street and Station Street. It was demolished in 1907 when the introduction of the tramway system made road widening necessary. This photograph was taken from the end of Station Street looking towards Nottingham Road and it gives a rare view of Albert Street before it was widened.

The Black Swan, Albert Street, seen in 1909. It once had a chequered career in the field of politics. In 1830 it was the headquarters of the Mansfield Reformers, supporters of the parliamentary reform bill. Nine years later, in 1839, it became the headquarters of the more militant Chartist Movement. It was rebuilt in 1925.

The Blue Bell Inn once stood in Church Street. It is seen here shortly before it was demolished in 1869 to make way for the railway viaduct. All the premises on this side of Church Street were partially dug out of the natural rock face into which they backed. The landlord of the inn was Mr George Parr, a well-known cricketer. He is said to have organized sparrow shoots to entertain his patrons.

Ye Olde Ramme Inne on Church Street is one of the town's oldest inns. During restoration work in 1987, items dating back to the sixteenth century were uncovered. Below is the inn following the restoration work, showing the new mock-Tudor-timbered façade. Sadly, the two dormer windows were not retained.

The yard of the Greyhound Hotel, 1890, formerly of Stockwell Gate. In common with other town centre hotels, it provided extensive stabling for its patrons, with accommodation for up to thirty horses. The yard was also used by a local carrier named Sutton who ran daily services to Clay Cross, South Normanton and Hucknall. The hotel was the headquarters of Mansfield's first cricket club in 1833. They were known as the 'peep-o-day' boys, because of the early hours in which they turned out for net practice. It was also the headquarters of the horticultural society who staged annual flower and gooseberry shows here.

Domestic

The Chapman and Carr families outside Little Matlock House in 1910 after a family wedding. Mr Chapman was manager at Little Matlock Cotton Mill.

Robert White, proprietor of the Swan Hotel, Church Street, was one of Mansfield's most respected citizens until his death in 1876. He is seen here in 1869 at the age of 62, with his second wife, Jane, his daughter, Anne Reid White (17), who was to die in 1873, his eldest son, John Harrop, seated right, and young Robert, standing left. This photograph was taken in Mansfield Cemetery (note the asphalt path) and is from a box of stereoscopic pictures ordered by Sarah Ann White, Mr White's daughter from his first marriage. John Harrop White appears in several photographs in this book.

A family tea taken alfresco in the early 1920s. The identities of the partakers, including the Brunts schoolboy, are not known but this appears to have been a lavish meal with a varied spread of scones, malt bread and cakes, the table decorated with flowers. All the younger ladies wear fashionable shady hats while the elderly lady at the end of the table favours a style dating from some years back.

The rock houses on Ratcliffe Gate were not unique as others existed elsewhere in Britain and also on the continent. In these ancient dwellings, large families of besom makers eked out a sparse lifestyle, although free from the burden of local taxes. Mischievous children used to creep into the field above the houses where the chimneys emerged and block them with stones. The last rock house was vacated in 1910, after the death of Mrs Charlotte Bramwell. During the Second World War, the caves were used as air-raid shelters.

Inside a rock house about 1900. This cramped living space was hollowed out by hand, and the natural sandstone whitewashed to lighten the dark interior. The occupant made slight attempts to create an illusion of comfort, laying a threadbare carpet, providing Windsor-style chairs (which appear to have received a recent coat of polish) and decorating the walls with prints, one of which is of a David Wilkie painting and the other a popular engraving of a rat pit with terriers.

Pensioners of Elizabeth Heath's Charity were more fortunate than those compelled to spend their declining years in the workhouse. Here a discussion is taking place at the pump, situated in the garden at the rear of the almshouses on Nottingham Road, although by 1900, the date of this photograph, it is probable that mains water was available to the twelve beneficiaries who received a small sum of money each month, a new gown yearly and a supply of coal. In earlier times Heath's pensioners were buried in the garden, then used as a graveyard, but only the grave of the founder, Elizabeth Heath, remains today.

Some Mansfield men were serving in South Africa in the Boer War when this young boy, in somewhat fanciful military dress and splendidly mounted on a fine rocking horse, was photographed at the back of his Duke Street home. No more than fifteen years later, with hundreds of his contemporaries from the town, he was undergoing the horrors and privations of the Western Front. Wounded, gassed, a prisoner of war, he finally returned home in 1919.

Mrs Phyllis Carr in her art deco style dining room at 'Avalon', Brick Kiln Lane, Mansfield, 1938. The Carrs, active members of St Peter's church, appear in other photographs in this book.

The staircase, Berry Hill Hall, in 1920, at the time of its sale by Mrs Hollins. The wall was covered with oil paintings and mezzotints of eighteenth-century portraits. The splendid wrought-iron stair balustrade has been destroyed by vandals while fireplaces and roofing lead have been stolen during the past few years during which the hall has stood empty.

SECTION TWELVE

Wartime

Forest Town children posing with an effigy of 'Kaiser Bill' which was later burnt during celebrations to mark the end of the First World War.

During the First World War khaki-clad troops were rarely absent from the streets of Mansfield. Almost without exception they came from a vast camp that had been established at nearby Clipstone. As early as 1915, in the first year of the war, rows of wooden huts were built and troops could be seen drilling and exercising in the heather-covered countryside. At its largest, upwards of 30,000 men were stationed there, about three-quarters of the population of Mansfield. Naturally, such an influx to the district had its impact. Local workmen helped construct the camp, local tradesmen supplied some of its needs and local people offered hospitality to the troops. Mansfield, too, was the natural venue for off-duty hours. Cafés, public houses and places of entertainment were inevitably popular while churches and chapels often numbered visiting soldiers among their congregations. After the war the camp was dismantled though some of the huts were retained and used as homes for the first miners at the colliery as well as temporary places of worship and schools. Even now one or two still survive.

Many local men served in the county regiment, the Sherwood Foresters, during the First World War. This group, which included some from Mansfield, formed the signals section of the 2nd, 8th battalion. The photograph was taken on 15 January 1918 during a respite from duty in the trenches on the Western Front. Within a fortnight the battalion had been disbanded and the men posted to other units of the brigade to bring them up to strength. No doubt the soldier on the left of the front row found active service at the front more rigorous than his earlier 'military' experience (see page 137).

Mansfield Patriotic Fair was held in Titchfield Park in June 1917. Twenty thousand visitors thronged the ground and the event realized several thousand pounds for the war effort. Here the Forest Town ladies pose in front of their tent, where china, earthenware and glass items were sold.

The YMCA forces canteen, 1915. The building on Church Lane was purchased by the YMCA in 1911. In 1915 it was adapted as a canteen and recreation centre for the large number of troops coming into the town from the Clipstone Camp. It was manned on a voluntary basis by local ladies, assisted by boy scouts.

Members of the 369 Company 42 S/L Regiment RE TA, in 1938, shortly before they were mobilized during the Munich crisis. Seen here from the left, back row: C. Carr, A. Woolley, T. Gale, S. Ball, H. Staples, P. Farmilo, -?-, -?-, -?-, Sgt Alf Clark. Second row: -?-, -?-, -?-, -?-, B. Lilliman, Carl Lee and, at the front, W. Gamble.

Mansfield escaped serious air raids during the Second World War though people's sleep was often broken by the drone of enemy bombers flying overhead. Perhaps it was the thought of hitting back at them that made the local Spitfire Fund so successful. Once launched, people were encouraged to raise £5,000 which was the cost of one of these aircraft. Mansfield's fund soon reached its target and the Spitfire on the photograph was duly named *Sherwood Forester*. It flew operationally for almost a year before being converted for photographic reconnaissance work. On 19 July 1953, while on a training flight in poor visibility, it crashed into a hillside on the Isle of Skye.

'Back your Boys' week in June 1941 concluded a six months' National Savings campaign in the town intended to raise half a million pounds to support the war effort. Processions, demonstrations and the visit of the First Lord of the Admiralty, the Rt Hon. A.V. Alexander, attracted crowds of spectators. Here the procession passes the Victoria Hotel in Albert Street.

A National Savings rally in the Market Place during 'Back your Boys' week in 1941. The appearance of this part of the town has changed very little since then, although the market stalls are now never removed and the surface has been relaid with bricks.

Farm Sunday, on 4 July 1943, transformed Mansfield into the agricultural centre it had been in the past, with the difference that the mile-long procession was mainly made up by machinery for use on the farm and only a few ancient horse-drawn wagons represented old times on the land. This photograph was taken in front of the Town Hall, where Ivy, Duchess of Portland, addressed a large crowd.

National Savings organizers and collectors attended a meeting at Queen Elizabeth's Girls' Grammar School on 18 March 1944 when an Air Ministry plaque and log books recording operational flights were presented by Wing Commander Selby-Lowndes. Centre front row are the mayor and mayoress of Mansfield, Councillor Ilion and Mrs Pickard.

Civil defence was a vital issue in 1954, when this photograph was taken in the newly opened Civil Defence Headquarters in Bath Street. In the group are Assistant Civil Defence Officer A. Blacklock, Contingent Leader J. Higgins, Head Warden S.G. Hudson, Assistant Chief Warden A.C. Shepherd, and Deputy Head Warden C. Carr.

Charter Celebrations in Mansfield began on 14 July 1891. This photograph shows the triumphal arch on Stockwell Gate, one of many erected in the town centre to celebrate the town's new status.

The Swainmote Dinner took place originally after the meeting of verderers in Sherwood Forest fifteen days before Holyrood day or Michaelmas. The feast was revived by the Old Mansfield Society in the 1920s and was held regularly, with the exception of the war years, until 1958. Traditional menus included roast swan, boar's head, venison pasties and syllabubs. This 1949 photograph, taken at the Swan Hotel, shows the entry of the boar's head, accompanied by dancing maidens singing the Boar's Head Carol. The girls were pupils of High Oakham School.

The opening of Mansfield's Electricity Works on 17 June 1903. The ceremony was performed by the mayor, Alderman John Crampton, and the chairman of the Electric Lighting Committee, Councillor W.J. Chadburn. A brass plate to commemorate the event was fixed at the Works and the Town Hall clock was changed from gas to electric illumination. Personalities in the photograph include Robert Barringer, J. Harrop White, J.E. Birks, Harry Smith and Timothy Taylor.

On Wednesday 6 July 1904 the foundation stone of Mansfield's Carnegie Library was laid by Mrs Markham, wife of Sir Arthur Markham, who was MP for the town. The Town Council had originally approached the Duke of Portland, but due to a prior commitment his Grace had declined to perform the ceremony. Mr Andrew Carnegie was then asked but refused, so Mrs Markham graciously stepped in. This ceremony was followed by that of the official opening of the adjacent Baily Museum by Mrs J.E. Alcock, wife of the mayor.

Mayor's Sunday, 13 November 1910. After Divine Service at St John's church, the mayoral party proceeded to the Town Hall, where this photograph was taken. Included in the group are the mayor, Alderman Timothy Taylor, deputy mayor, Councillor John Collins, Revd Mr Lilley, mayor's chaplain, and Mr John Harrop White, town clerk. Mayor's Sunday took place every year after the mayor-making ceremony.

Hoisting the flag presented by the children of Mansfield, Victoria, Australia on 8 October 1909. Five thousand schoolchildren assembled in front of the Town Hall to witness the ceremony, which was marred by bad weather. The flag from this gold-mining district, where the Ned Kelly gang had operated in the 1870s, was worked with an inscription, 'From the children of Mansfield, Australia, to the children of Mansfield, England, 1909'. A Union Jack, along with photographs of the ceremony, were sent to Australia as a gesture of thanks.

Little normal work was done and few people stayed at home on the morning of 25 June 1914 when King George V and Queen Mary visited Mansfield. The weather was favourable and the sun shone on the 8,000 children who lined the route, the crowd that packed the Market Place, the 600 policemen on duty and the local territorial army units who formed a guard of honour and added a splash of colour and military pageantry to the scene. At 11.33 the King and Queen mounted a specially erected dais that stood in front of the Town Hall. Here they were welcomed by the mayor, Alderman J. Taylor, and his grand-daughter, Constance Leila Taylor, presented a bouquet to the Queen. The King was asked to open the King Edward Memorial Wing of the hospital formally. After a few appropriate words, he pressed a button and the hospital doors swung open. The royal visitors then drove to Barringer, Wallis & Manners metal-box factory where they spent some time.

Mansfield's Women's Suffragette Society had seventy members when this photograph was taken in 1910. Monthly meetings were held at Miss Eileen Barringer's house, 'Edenwood', on Crow Hill Drive. Although officially allied to the UWSS, the Mansfield branch was non-militant and non-party. The local president was Miss Wright, the secretary, Mrs Manners, and the treasurer, Miss Barringer.

Mrs Mary Ellen Marriott, mayor of Mansfield, opening the new museum on 19 October 1938. The old museum, the 'Tin Tabernacle' donated to the town in 1904 by William Edward Baily, then the majority shareholder in Mansfield Brewery, had deteriorated to such an extent that it had had to be closed and demolished nearly three years earlier.

Reception of the Prince of Wales, 1 August 1923. After a short ceremony, the Prince strolled past the crowds of children, singling out and shaking hands with the headmaster of Moor Lane School, Mr A.H. Gelsthorpe, who was wearing a badge of the Welsh Guards Comrades Club, of which regiment the Prince was Honorary Colonel. Before he left, the Prince asked the mayor, Henry Daniel, to grant a school holiday in honour of the occasion.

Market Charter celebrations were held in July 1927 to mark the 500th anniversary of the granting of a charter by Richard II allowing the men of Mansfield and their heirs to hold a fair in perpetuity. Here the mayor, Alderman D.H. Maltby, poses with officials and visitors on the Town Hall steps after attending a civic service in the parish church.

The Mansfield Hospital Carnival of 1932. A popular feature of the Carnival that year was an Elizabethan market set around the Old Market Cross on Westgate. All the participants dressed in Elizabethan costume, and the attractions included an old English inn and sedan chairs. Here, sampling the old English brew, is the mayor and mayoress, Councillor and Mrs Pollard, Mr A.S. Buxton and Mr J. Harrop White.

The unveiling of the Thompson Memorial, which was erected over the grave of Charles Thompson on Southwell Road, took place on 17 September 1932. The ceremony was performed by Alderman J. Beck, the chairman of the Brunts Charity, followed by the dedication by the Bishop of Southwell. Also present were the mayor and mayoress, Councillor and Mrs Pollard and the Revd C.R. Cotter of St Peter's church.

Mansfield Civic Service, 1971, was held at St Peter's church. The mayor that year was Councillor Groves, a popular member of the council and of the RAF Association, having served as a crew member in bombers in the last war. Pictured from the left: Mr T. Rutland RBL, Councillor Groves MBE (the mayor), Mr S.W.R. Christmas (town clerk), Canon Warburton MBE (mayor's chaplain), Mr J. Scott and Mr F.W. Patmore (churchwardens), Mrs Belcher RBL, and Mr F.W. Pothecary (Sherwood Foresters).

Remembrance Day Parade, 1967. The familiar sight of the annual parade of ex-service veterans, as they march down Church Street, preceded by the Standards of the various ex-service organizations. The standard-bearers here are: Mr R. Belcher RBL (Sherwood Foresters), Mr F.W. Pothecary, Mrs Bennett RBL (women's section), followed by Mr B. Smith, Mr Pritchard DCM, Mr Musson TD and Mr Mills MM.

The pipes and drums of the Seaforth Highlanders Association leading the annual Remembrance Day Parade in 1991. The association was formed in 1966 by a small group of veterans from the regiment, two of them being Mr L. Pallet and Mr G. Priest. The band is made up of members from all walks of life and trades and is based in Pleasley.

St Mark's Henley Memorial Hall is dedicated to the memory of the Revd A.G. Henley, a former vicar of St Mark's, who was drowned in tragic circumstances on 5 August 1904. It was opened on 23 October 1909 by the Revd Lowndes Day, Canon A.H. Prior of St Peter's and the Revd W. Lilley of St John's. This is a retouched photograph which does not show the clerestory windows.

Centre Tree, Westgate. The Centre Tree, so named for its supposed position in the centre of Sherwood Forest, was of course nothing of the sort. Its reputation as such appears to owe more to some nineteenth-century attempt at tourist promotion than to geographical fact. The tree pictured above stood until 1940 when it was deemed a traffic hazard and felled, the railings being used for scrap. Pictured below is the semi-mature oak being planted in the same spot in 1988 by the chairman of Mansfield District Council, Mrs Lorna Carter.

The War Memorial at Carr Bank Park was unveiled on 4 August 1921 and dedicated by the Bishop of Southwell to those men of Mansfield who gave their lives in the First World War. It was erected, to a design by Mr A.S. Buxton, in an attractive setting in a once beautiful park. Sadly, today it stands in a neglected state, its bronze wreaths and additional plaque dedicated to those who fell in the Second World War, torn from the walls and stolen. Nearby is a second memorial, dedicated to the men of the Sherwood Foresters Regiment who fell in the two world wars. This photograph shows the annual wreath-laying ceremony on Remembrance Day, 1990, watched by Canon Warburton.

Forest Town Boys Brigade parading through the village behind the Mansfield Colliery band. A drill hall was built in the village by the Bolsover Co. for the brigade. It was opened on 15 May 1909 by the Attorney General, Sir William Robson KC, MP, and Mr Emerson Bainbridge of the Bolsover Co.

Acknowledgements

We would like to acknowledge with thanks the following organizations and individuals, without whose help this collection would not have been possible:

The Old Mansfield Society • Mansfield Museum • Mansfield Library, Local Studies Section • Mansfield Chronicle Advertiser • Mansfield Brewery Co. CMB Promotional Packaging • Gordon Howlett Photography • Mr D. Bradbury Mrs K. Baugh • Mrs E. Carlin • The late Mr C. Carr • Miss E. Chatterton Mrs Roma (?) Crowe • Mr A. Coupe • Mr and Mrs A. Curtiss Miss E. Downing • Miss V. Drakes • Mrs N. Dugdale • Major T.S. Martin Mr L. Orton • Miss D. Pothecary • Mr J. Purdy • Mrs S. Stevens Mrs H. Straw • Mr S. Waller